The Let's Talk Library

Let's Talk About
Being Afraid

Anna Kreiner

The Rosen Publishing Group's
PowerKids Press™
New York

Published in 1996, 2004 by The Rosen Publishing Group, Inc.
29 East 21st Street, New York, NY 10010

Revised Edition 2004

Editor: Jennifer Way
Book Design: Erin McKenna
Text Revisions: Gillian Houghton

Photo Credits: Cover, pp. 4, 8, 15 by Maura B. McConnell; p. 7 © Chuck Mason/International Stock; pp. 11, 12 © Scott Thode/International Stock; p. 20 © John Michael/International Stock; p. 16 © Jeff Greenberg/International Stock; p. 19 © Chad Ehlers/International Stock.

Kreiner, Anna.
    Let's talk about being afraid / Anna Kreiner.
          p.   cm. — (The let's talk library)
    Includes index.
    Summary: A simple introduction to what causes fear and how to handle being afraid.
    ISBN 0-8239-6930-4
    1. Fear in children. [1. Fear.] I. Title. II. Series
BF723.F4K73 1996
155.4'1246—dc20   96-48382
                                                            CIP
                                                            AC

Manufactured in the United States of America

Table of Contents

What Are You Afraid Of?

Are you afraid of the dark? Do ghost stories give you scary dreams? Are you afraid to go down into the basement or up into the attic? Do bugs make your skin crawl? Are you afraid when your parents fight?

Everyone feels afraid sometimes. Even grown-ups get scared. When you feel afraid, you worry that something bad will happen to you or to someone that you know or love.

◀ People are afraid of many different things. For a boy who is afraid of deep water, a trip to the swimming pool can be very scary.

Fear

Being afraid means feeling fear. Fear is an **emotion**. Happiness, sadness, and anger are also emotions. Everyone feels these emotions sometimes, including your mom or dad.

Fear is not a bad emotion. It can help to keep you safe. Too much fear can be unhealthy. Fear can prevent you from doing fun things, such as making new friends. Fear can also keep you from doing things that are good for you, such as going to the doctor.

Talking about your fears is an important step in dealing with them. ▶

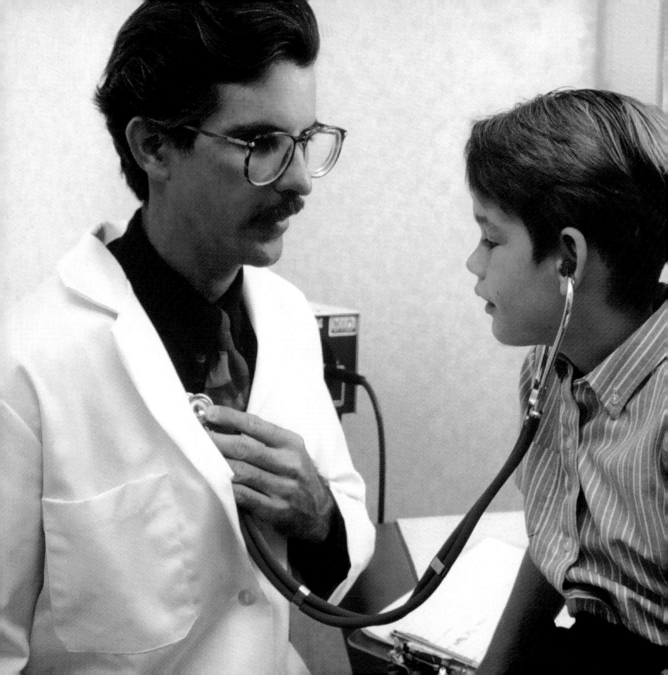

Knowing When You Are Afraid

Your body usually tells you when you are afraid. Your heart begins to beat faster. You may have trouble swallowing. You may feel "butterflies" in your stomach. You feel this way because your body is preparing for you either to fight against or to run from what you fear. This **response** is normal. Scientists call it the fight-or-flight response. It is how your body **protects** you and prepares you for **situations** that might hurt you.

◀ Your body lets you know when you feel afraid. Your body's response protects you from danger.

Why Are You Afraid?

Sometimes you know why you are afraid. Maybe you were bitten by a dog when you were younger, and now you are scared of dogs. You may have seen a scary television show about a clown, and now you do not like clowns. It is okay to be afraid of these kinds of things.

Other times you may not know why you are afraid. You may not know why thunder scares you. It is still okay to be afraid.

Many people think clowns are scary, and many people think clowns are funny. ▶

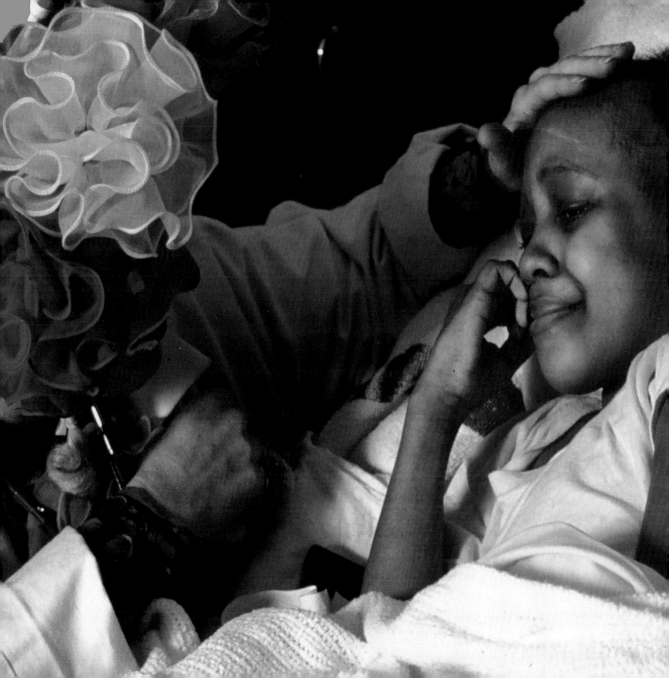

Special Kinds of Fear

Really strong feelings of fear are called **phobias**. Someone who is scared of high places has **acrophobia**. A person who is afraid of being in a small space has **claustrophobia**. Some people live their whole lives being afraid of heights or small spaces.

You probably do not have a phobia, but you may have fears. There are things you can do to help make your fears go away.

◀ You probably do not have acrophobia, but you may sometimes be afraid of heights.

Things That Have Hurt You

Sometimes you are afraid of things that have hurt you, such as a dog that bites, or a hot stove. These fears may keep you from getting hurt again. If you are afraid of getting burned again, you will not touch a hot stove. Knowing that these fears can be helpful does not make feeling them any easier. Tell your parents, a teacher, or a good friend how you are feeling. Just knowing that somebody else knows and cares can help to make you feel better.

14

Talking to a parent may help you to face your fear. ▶

Imaginary Creatures

You may be afraid of **imaginary** creatures, such as monsters or ghosts. Here are two ways to deal with these fears.

- Try to understand that these creatures cannot hurt you because they cannot touch you. They only exist in your imagination.
- Describe the creature to yourself, but imagine that the scary monster is actually a friendly monster who helps you.

◀ Your brother or sister may be able to help you imagine and describe a friendly monster.

New Things

You may be afraid of new things, such as moving to a new neighborhood or going to a new school. You may be afraid that you will not make friends or that you will get lost in your new building. Work through these fears by preparing for the new situation. Ask your parents to take you to meet your new teacher. See if there are any other kids in your new neighborhood or building. Doing something to prepare yourself will help to lessen your fears.

Ask your mom to take you for a walk in your new neighborhood. ▶

Things You Cannot Change

You may have heard about a war on television. Perhaps someone broke into your neighbor's house. Maybe someone you know was hurt. You may be afraid that these things may happen to you or someone you love.

Tell your parents or a teacher how you feel. They may not be able to keep these things from happening, but they can help to keep you as safe as possible. Knowing that they understand may make you feel better.

◀ **Your parents want to keep you safe and happy.**

It Is Okay to Be Afraid

It is okay to be scared. Everyone is afraid sometimes. You cannot always make your fears go away. However, you can take care of yourself by talking to other people about your fears. You may find that someone else has some of the same fears that you do. You can help each other by talking about them.

Glossary

acrophobia (a-kruh-FOH-bee-uh) A strong fear of high places.

claustrophobia (klos-truh-FOH-bee-uh) A strong fear of being in small spaces.

emotion (ih-MOH-shun) A feeling.

imaginary (ih-MA-jih-ner-ee) Made up.

phobias (FOH-bee-uz) Strong fears.

protects (pruh-TEKTS) Keeps from harm.

response (rih-SPONS) An action or a feeling caused by something such as another action, a sight, or a sound.

situations (sih-choo-AY-shunz) Problems or events.

Index

Web Sites

Due to the changing nature of Internet links, PowerKids Press has developed an online list of Web sites related to the subject of this book. This site is updated regularly. Please use this link to access the list: www.powerkidslinks.com/ltl/afraid/